The Children's Forest

PIONEER EDITION

By Peter Winkler

CONTENTS

2 Children in Charge

6 Explore South America

8 Rain Forests of the World

12 Concept Check

Kid Power. *This girl was one of the first leaders of the Children's Forest.*

Children in Charge

Kids in Peru have a special job. They take care of a forest. It's their own rain forest. They own it.

By Peter Winkler

Earth has big problems. People make too much **pollution.** This hurts Earth's air. It hurts its land. It hurts its water. Forests are getting smaller. Some animals are dying out.

Many people try to fix these problems. Joaquín Leguía (HWA keen luh GWEE uh) is one of them. He does **conservation** work. That means he protects Earth. He protects plants, animals, and wild places.

Leguía thinks kids can help. They might save the planet. How?

He thinks kids should own land. They can explore it. They can learn about it. They can find ways to protect Earth.

Getting Around. *Indian children are in a canoe. It's made from a tree trunk.*

Getting Land

In 2001 Leugia talked with people in southeastern Peru. Peru is a country in South America.

Leguía asked them a big question. Would they give part of their land to children?

The people said no. They did not want to give away land. They needed it. They needed it for hunting. They needed it for finding food.

Then the people changed their minds. They gave kids a big piece of land. That land is now called the Children's Forest.

Rain Forests

What kind of land? **A rain forest!** A rain forest is filled with trees. It gets at least four inches of rain each month. Most rain forests are warm all year. Many different kinds of plants and animals live in them.

Welcome to Our World. *RIGHT: Kids in Peru made this sign. The red shows a trail they made. The green words say "Children's Forest" in Spanish.*

Kids at Work

Taking care of a rain forest is a big job. How do the kids do it? They have meetings. They think of ideas. They ask teachers for help. They ask park rangers for help, too. Then they work hard.

The kids make trails. They make signs, too. Now they can explore the forest. And they won't get lost.

The kids study the animals. They made a nature guide. It tells about the forest plants. They learn how to earn money. They sell crafts. They make them from nuts and leaves.

The children are doing what Leguía had hoped. They explore their land. They take care of it. They have learned to love it, too.

© JAY DICKMAN, CORBIS (BOAT); © THEO ALLOFS CORBIS (BIRD); JOAQUIN LEGUIA (KIDS, FISH)

Wordwise

conservation: protecting Earth's places, plants, and animals

pollution: anything that harms air, land, or water

rain forest: wooded area that gets at least four inches of rain each month

Wild Place. *LEFT: This is a scarlet macaw. It lives in the rain forest. It is just one of many rain forest animals. Humans are still learning what animals live in rain forests.*

5

Explore South America

South America has rain forests. It has deserts. It has mountains. It has grasslands. South America has the world's longest mountain range. It has the Amazon River. Search the map. See these features of South America.

Got Trees? *This is a brown capuchin monkey. He's on a tree branch. Many kinds of monkeys live in South America's forests.*

Lost World. *A cactus grows near Peru's coast. It is dry there. Behind is an ancient city. No one lives there now.*

Winter Coats. *Alpacas have thick hair. It keeps them warm.*

North
America

South
America

EQUATOR

VENEZUELA

SURINAME

FRENCH
GUIANA
(France)

GUYANA

COLOMBIA

ECUADOR

Amazon River

Amazon River

P E R U

B R A Z I L

BOLIVIA

PACIFIC
OCEAN

PARAGUAY

ATLANTIC
OCEAN

C H I L E

A R G E N T I N A

URUGUAY

N
W   E
S

Falkland Islands
(United Kingdom)

Map Key

Mountain

Desert

Rain forest

Grassland

Wetland

Rain Forests

Earth has two kinds of rain forests. How are they alike? How are they different?

Tropical Rain Forests

Most rain forests are tropical. They are near the Equator. That is an area around the center of Earth. Tropical rain forests are warm all year.

These forests get a lot of rain. Some get 400 inches of rain in a year!

Tropical rain forests are full of life. The trees are thick. Vines twist up the trees. Plants are everywhere.

Many kinds of animals live in the forests. Monkeys swing in branches. Insects buzz. Birds are in the trees. Animals are everywhere.

Tropical rain forests are only a small part of the planet. But half of Earth's plants and animals live in them.

At Home in the Heat.
ABOVE: This gorilla lives in a tropical rain forest. RIGHT: This African rain forest is full of plants.

Tropical Rain Forests

Rainfall Tropical rain forests get between 80 and 400 inches of rain a year!

Location Almost all tropical rain forests are near the Equator. They are warm all year long.

Fun Fact The Amazon rain forest is in South America. It is the world's largest tropical rain forest. More kinds of plants and animals live there than anywhere else on Earth.

MICHAEL NICHOLS/NATIONAL GEOGRAPHIC STOCK

Temperate Rain Forests

Temperate rain forests are different from tropical ones. How? They are farther from the Equator. They are warm in summer. But they are cool in winter.

Temperate rain forests get less rain than tropical ones. Most get about 100 inches of rain a year. They have fewer kinds of plants and animals, too.

Many plants and animals live in temperate forests. Mosses and ferns cover the forest floor. Redwood trees grow hundreds of feet tall. Squirrels leap in treetops. Marmots and deer nibble plants. Temperate rain forests are homes to many living things.

Getting Along in the Forest.
ABOVE: These marmots live in a temperate rain forest. *RIGHT:* This temperate rain forest is in California. Much of its rain comes from thick ocean fog.

The Future of Forests

Rain forests are filled with life. But they are in danger. People cut down more forests every year. This is bad for plants, animals, and people, too.

Many kinds of living things depend on rain forests. That is why projects like the Children's Forest are important. They help save Earth's rain forests.

Temperate Rain Forests

Rainfall Temperate rain forests get about 100 inches of rain a year.

Location Most temperate rain forests are near the western coasts of North America and South America.

Fun Fact Trees in temperate rain forests usually live longer than trees in tropical rain forests. Giant sequoias can live thousands of years.

Rain Forests

Answer these questions to find out what you have learned.

1 What is conservation?

2 Why does Leguía think children should own land?

3 What is the Children's Forest?

4 What did kids learn from the Children's Forest?

5 How are the two kinds of rain forests alike? How are they different?